DINÉ

Heather Bruegl

21st Century
Junior Library

Indigenous Peoples
of North America

Published in the United States of America by:

CHERRY LAKE PRESS
2395 South Huron Parkway, Suite 200, Ann Arbor, Michigan 48104
www.cherrylakepress.com

Reading Adviser: Beth Walker Gambro, MS, Ed., Reading Consultant, Yorkville, IL

Cherry Lake Press is an imprint of Cherry Lake Publishing Group.

Library of Congress Cataloging-in-Publication Data

Names: Bruegl, Heather, author.
Title: Diné / written by: Heather Bruegl.
Description: Ann Arbor, MI : Cherry Lake Publishing, [2025] | Series:
   Indigenous peoples of North America | Includes bibliographical references and index. | Audience: Grades 2-3 | Summary:
   "The Diné, or Navajo, have made this continent their home for centuries. Today, Navajo Nation is the largest tribal nation
   in the United States. In this introduction, readers will learn about Diné people, land, history, and accomplishments. Written
   by Indigenous author and public historian, Heather Bruegl, a citizen of the Oneida Nation and first-line descendent
   Strockbridge-Munsee, this series provides a simple and authentic introduction to the unique cultures and peoples that
   have made this continent home for thousands of years, and are still here today"—
   Provided by publisher.
Identifiers: LCCN 2024036513 | ISBN 9781668956250 (hardcover) | ISBN
   9781668957103 (paperback) | ISBN 9781668957974 (ebook) | ISBN
   9781668958841 (pdf)
Subjects: LCSH: Navajo Indians—Juvenile literature.
Classification: LCC E99.N3 B746 2025 | DDC 979.1004/9726—dc23/eng/20240926
LC record available at https://lccn.loc.gov/2024036513

Cherry Lake Publishing would like to acknowledge the work of the Partnership for 21st Century Learning, a network of Battelle for Kids. Please visit Battelle for Kids online for more information.

Printed in the United States of America

Note from publisher: Websites change regularly, and their future contents are outside of our control.
Supervise children when conducting any recommended online searches for extended learning opportunities.

About the Cover: Jones Benally is a Diné elder, traditional healer, and world-champion hoop dancer. His daughter, Jeneda Benally, learned traditional medicine from him and is also a hoop dancer and musician. The cover shows them with other members of their family, including Benally's granddaughters Dyatihi and Deezchiil Benally, when they were featured in a *Las Vegas Review-Journal* article about the COVID pandemic's effect on Diné people. The family band, Sihasan, as well as the Jones Family Navajo Dance Troupe, perform around the world. Members also give lectures and presentations to schools and community organizations on Diné culture and traditional knowledge.

CONTENTS

WHO WE ARE

The Diné people are most often called Navajo. The word *Navajo* was used by Spanish explorers. They borrowed the word from the Tewas people. The Tewas word *navahu* meant "fields next to a valley." The Tewas told the Spanish about the Diné and where they lived. The Spanish named the Diné *Navajo*. The name is still used today. The nation is officially called Navajo Nation. But the people call themselves Diné. It means "the people."

Dr. Germaine Daye works with the USDA on the Safeguarding Natural Heritage Program at Navajo Technical University.

5

The Diné thrived for thousands of years in the Southwest. And they still do today. The Diné are the largest group of Indigenous people in the United States. Diné language is called *Diné Bizaad*. Around 175,000 people speak it in the

Diné traditions are passed down to the next generation.

Think!

Why might people want to increase the number of people who speak Diné?

United States. That number used to be higher. Fewer young people speak it. Language programs hope to change that.

Within the nation are many communities and clans. The clans build family connections. They help strengthen relationships. Like many other tribal nations, the Diné value balance in the mind, body, and spirit. Diné culture includes many ceremonies. Through rituals, the Diné work to stay balanced and in harmony.

OUR LIVES TODAY

More than 100,000 Diné live on their reservation. This reservation is the largest in the United States. It covers the Four Corners. That area is where Colorado, Utah, New Mexico, and Arizona meet. The land is often called Navajoland. It covers 27,413 square miles (71,000 square kilometers). Navajoland is larger than 10 different U.S. states.

Diné people are a diverse and important part of American life. They work as teachers, doctors, actors, lawyers, scientists, and all jobs in between. They are athletes, artists, writers, and politicians.

Di'Orr Greenwood is a Diné skateboarder and artist. Her work was featured on U.S. stamps celebrating skateboarding.

Rowan Espino was a Diné intern with Banfield Pet Hospital in Los Angeles County.

Create!

Make a poster describing Diné government today. With an adult, go online to find out about Diné leaders and government departments. Tell how it is like a state or national government. Tell how it is different.

Diné people include baseball player Jacoby Ellsbury and weaver D.Y. Begay. They also include writer and environmentalist Elizabeth Woody and Arizona State Representative Albert Hale.

The **Navajo Code Talkers** who served during World War II (1939–1945) are probably the most famous Diné. The Code Talkers were instrumental during the war. They used the Diné language to send coded messages. Their code was never broken. It gave the U.S. military an important advantage. The Code Talkers helped win the war.

Look at this picture of Diné land. What do you see? What do you think the climate is like?

OUR ANCESTRAL LANDS

Diné homelands are called Dinéhtah. Before **first contact**, their land mass was centered within the four **sacred** mountains. These are Blanca Peak and Hesperus Peak in Colorado, Mount Taylor in New Mexico, and San Francisco Peaks in Arizona.

The Diné's relationship with the land is important. So is their relationship with water. Water is a precious resource. It is sacred. The Diné grew the **Three Sisters**, which are corn, beans, and squash. They were also ranchers. They kept herds of cattle and sheep. They wove woolen **textiles** like blankets, rugs, and clothes. These textiles are still made today.

In the 1860s, the U.S. military forced the Diné to leave their land. This was called the Long Walk. It included about 53 forced marches. Around 10,000 Diné took the Long Walk. Afterward, the Diné were forced to live in **internment** camps. Disease and starvation killed 3,500 people. In 1868, the Diné signed the Treaty of Bosque Redondo. This agreement freed the captive Diné. They returned to their ancestral land.

Weavers helped the Diné survive internment and preserve traditions.

Ask Questions!

What other major American events were taking place in the 1860s? Ask a librarian, teacher, or other adult to help you find answers.

Today, the Diné reservation lies on that ancestral land. But outside influence can cause problems. Clean water can be hard to get. The Navajo Water Project says that 30 percent of people on the reservation do not have access to it. Many families must travel for miles to get water. Then they must use what they get all week long.

Uranium mining on Diné land caused the water shortage. Uranium is a type of metal. Non-Indigenous companies mined uranium from the 1940s to the 1980s. This polluted the water. It became undrinkable. The Diné people work to repair the damage and restore their land and water.

A Diné worker at Monument Valley Navajo Tribal Park in Arizona works to care for the sacred land.

CARRYING TRADITIONS FORWARD

Diné history and teachings are passed down through **oral tradition**. Teachings and ceremonies are held sacred. The land has meaning. Holy places on that land are important.

In Diné traditions, the world we live in now is the Fourth World. The Diné passed through three other worlds before this one. The number four is present throughout their teachings. There are the four directions, four seasons, the original four clans, and four sacred mountains.

The Diné way of life has much meaning. Even their tribal flag has important symbolism. The copper outline shows the original boundaries of the reservation. The current land is shown in dark brown. Mountain symbols for the four sacred mountains mark north, east, south, and west. The rainbow symbolizes sovereignty. The sun is shown above two green stalks of corn. They surround a traditional hogan and modern home. Other symbols represent animals as well as industry. The flag shows the past and present of the Diné. It also shows their future potential.

Make a Guess!

Look at the image of the Navajo Nation flag. Why do you think these symbols were chosen? Why are they important?

GLOSSARY

clans (KLANZ) groups of people connected by a common ancestor

first contact (FERST KAHN-takt) the time when Indigenous peoples first met Europeans

hogan (HOH-guhn) traditional home or dwelling of the Diné people

internment (in-TERN-muhnt) imprisonment for political or military reasons

Navajo Code Talkers (NAH-vuh-hoh KOHD TAW-kerz) a group of U.S. Marines who served during World War II and helped code and decode messages for the military

oral tradition (OR-uhl truh-DIH-shuhn) verbal accounts of history, songs, and languages and how these are passed down

reservation (reh-zer-VAY-shuhn) a legally designated plot of land held in trust for Indigenous peoples by the U.S. federal government

rituals (RIH-chuh-wuhlz) acts performed in a set order or manner, such as parts of a ceremony

sacred (SAY-kruhd) holy; important to a system of belief

sovereignty (SAH-vruhn-tee) freedom from outside rule or control

symbolism (SIM-buh-lih-zuhm) the use of images to represent larger ideas

textiles (TEK-stylz) cloth goods that are usually woven or knit

Three Sisters (THREE SIH-sterz) a form of planting in Indigenous communities that refers to the planting of corn, beans, and squash

FIND OUT MORE

Books

Bruegl, Heather. *Indigenous Peoples and Military Service*. Ann Arbor, MI: Cherry Lake Press, 2024

Sorell, Traci. *We Are Grateful: Otsaliheliga*. Watertown, MA: Charlesbridge, 2021.

Sorell, Traci. *We Are Still Here! Native American Truths Everyone Should Know*. Watertown, MA: Charlesbridge, 2021.

Online

With an adult, explore more online with these suggested searches.

- "Navajo Arts," Discover Navajo
- "The Hogan," Discover Navajo

Say Hello!

Yá'át'ééh (yaht-AY) is a Diné greeting. It means "it's good" and more deeply, "everything on the surface of Mother Earth and in my life is good."

INDEX

ABOUT THE AUTHOR

Heather Bruegl, a member of the Oneida Nation of Wisconsin/Stockbridge-Munsee, is a Madonna University graduate with a Master of Arts in U.S. History. She is a public historian and decolonial educator, and her Munsee name is Kiishookunkwe, which means "Sunflower in Full Bloom." Heather frequently travels to present on Indigenous history, policy, and activism, bringing her deep knowledge and personal connection to the subject.